VISIBLE LIVING

OTHER BOOKS BY
MARYA FIAMENGO

The Quality of Halves (1958)

Overheard at the Oracle (1969)

Silt of Iron (1971)

In Praise of Old Women (1976)

North of the Cold Star (1978)

Patience after Compline (1989)

White Linen Remembered (1996)

Visible living

POEMS SELECTED AND NEW

For Patricia
with much love

Marya Fiamengo

Marya Fiamengo

Edited by Janice Fiamengo,
Seymour Mayne & Russell Thornton

RONSDALE PRESS

VISIBLE LIVING
Copyright © 2006 Marya Fiamengo

RONSDALE PRESS
3350 West 21st Avenue
Vancouver, B.C., Canada V6S 1G7
www.ronsdalepress.com

Typesetting: Julie Cochrane, in New Baskerville 11 pt on 13.5
Cover Design: Julie Cochrane
Cover Art: Joe Plaskett, "Marya Fiamengo"
Paper: Ancient Forest Friendly Rolland "Enviro" — 100% post-consumer
    waste, totally chlorine-free and acid-free

Ronsdale Press wishes to thank the following for their support of its publishing program: the Canada Council for the Arts, the Government of Canada through the Book Publishing Industry Development Program (BPIDP), and the Province of British Columbia through the Book Publishing Tax Credit program and the British Columbia Arts Council.

Library and Archives Canada Cataloguing in Publication

Fiamengo, Marya
    Visible living: poems selected and new / Marya Fiamengo; edited by Janice Fiamengo, Seymour Mayne & Russell Thornton.

ISBN-13: 978-1-55380-042-2
ISBN-10: 1-55380-042-7

    I. Fiamengo, Janice Anne, 1964–   II. Mayne, Seymour, 1944–
III. Thornton, Russell IV. Title.

PS8511.I2V48 2006   C811'.54   C2006-903844-9

At Ronsdale Press we are committed to protecting the environment. To this end we are working with Markets Initiative (www.oldgrowthfree.com) and printers to phase out our use of paper produced from ancient forests. This book is one step towards that goal.

Printed in Canada by Hignell Printing, Winnipeg

dedicated to the memory of my parents,
Jakov and Matija Fiamengo,
and to the entire
Dalmatian-Canadian community
in which I was raised

ACKNOWLEDGEMENTS

I would like to thank the publishers and editors
of my previous books for their help and belief in my work.

CONTENTS

PREFACE

Right from the beginning, Marya Fiamengo has lived her life in two languages and two cultures. From her Slavic background stems her attraction to epic heroism, her respect for women's wisdom, and her long-standing interest in European history; from her Anglo-Canadian inheritance, she developed a love for Red Tory ideals of social justice, political stability, and sympathy for the oppressed as well as a suspicion of capitalist excesses. Her distinctive poetic voice blends the passion and lyricism of her ancestral language and mythos with the decorum, historical resonance, and moral commitments (sometimes expressed in satire and invective) of the British and Canadian traditions. Her commitment to their interweaving is a keynote of her poetic achievement

Born in 1926, the eldest child of immigrants from the Croatian island of Vis, Fiamengo grew up speaking Croatian and having to translate and conduct transactions for her parents, a duty that forced the shy and inward-looking child into early self-reliance and verbal dexterity. Drawn to books, immersing herself in Shakespeare, Greek tragedy, and Victorian literature in her early teens, she was determined at that time to become a novelist. While pursuing her Bachelor's degree in English literature at the University of British Columbia, she was introduced to *Beowulf* and was impressed by the heroic ethos, for which she felt an instinctive affinity. At this time also, she met Mary Plaskett, sister of the painter Joseph Plaskett, who introduced her to his friend Jack Hardman, an artist and sculptor. After completing her BA, she and Jack married and travelled to the Dalmatian Coast of Yugoslavia and then to England, where they spent a year teaching. Returning to the Vancouver area, she worked as a librarian and then bore a son, Dmitri. When her marriage ended in divorce, she returned to UBC in the early 1960s to complete a Master's degree in English and Creative Writing under the direction of Earle Birney and Dorothy Livesay; she lived in North Burnaby and then, after taking up a teaching post at UBC, in West Vancouver. She taught in the English department from 1962 to 1993, publishing seven volumes of poetry as well as numerous critical reviews and essays. Throughout her career she was a committed advocate of Canadian cultural and national autonomy. She now lives in Gibsons, BC, on the Sunshine Coast, where she continues to write poetry and to lobby the government on issues of culture and social justice.

Fiamengo began writing poetry in the 1950s, at a time when Vancouver was becoming a centre of literary and artistic activity. Earle Birney and Dorothy Livesay were two leading figures in the literary community, acclaimed poets who expressed their socialist commitments in poetry employing unconventional verse forms, Imagist techniques, and a bold demotic language. At the same time, a group of writers, many of them not yet published, met regularly to read their work and discuss art and culture. Mainly organized by William and Alice McConnell, the group included, at different times, Doris and Jack Shadbolt, Anne Marriott, Robert Harlow, Alice Munro, Phyllis Webb, and Jane Rule. Fiamengo became a part of this group and was encouraged by group members to submit to *Contemporary Verse*, a pioneer literary journal dedicated to new Canadian writing; it had been established in 1941 by Alan Crawley and regularly published work by Livesay, Birney, A.J.M. Smith, Anne Wilkinson, P.K. Page, Daryl Hine, and Fred Cogswell. Fiamengo's first poems were published in *Contemporary Verse* in 1952.

By 1958, Fiamengo had established herself as a presence on the West Coast poetry scene with the publication of *The Quality of Halves*. This volume was the first publication of Klanak Press, a small publishing house dedicated to careful craftsmanship, founded by Bill and Alice McConnell in that year. The poems, with their frequent mythic allusions, lavishly surreal images, and mystical, highly suggestive language, show affinities with Canadian mythopoeic poets such as Phyllis Webb and Jay MacPherson. The influence of Yeats's work, especially in the references to Byzantium, is also evident. Symbolic density and elusive metaphors combine to create haunting and evocative passages. The voice in these poems is at once intimate and oracular, speaking of visions, premonitions, longing and recollection. In one of the best of the poems, "Poem for Sarajevo," the speaker expresses her sense of being inhabited by a distant yet powerfully felt ancestry:

For there in that hall of mountains I could hear
the murmurous, brothering destiny of the flesh that
          clothes my bones
and I, no longer I, but all my mothering fathering tribe
beat instant with the pulse, was water with the voicing
                flood
which throbbed and flowed incessant circles around my
                being

Throughout, the speaker is interested in the psychic and emotive force of landscapes, the way we carry place and time within us. Unlike the logician whom she mocks in "The Logician, His System," she is entranced by "languages / you can't explain" as the "keys to everlastingness." For her, poetry is a "breath of mist /

to mute the harshness of impermanence" ("Epithalamium"). The power of poetry to overcome "impermanence" will be a lasting theme in Fiamengo's writing.

Silt of Iron (1971), her next full-length collection, was published by Ingluvin Publications; it is another beautiful small-press production, this one distinguished by the inclusion of drawings by Jack Shadbolt, already an internationally renowned artist. In the 1960s, Marya had established a close friendship with Seymour Mayne and Patrick Lane, two younger poets; Mayne and Lane had together helped to found Very Stone House, the press which had published a broadsheet of her poems entitled *Overheard at the Oracle* (1969). The *Oracle* poems were reprinted in *Silt of Iron* along with a variety of others, with the result that the volume gives evidence of stylistic change during the period of the late 1960s and early 1970s. The break with the poems in *The Quality of Halves* is immediately apparent. Although myth remains a primary focus, the lavish imagery and dense language has been significantly pared down. A number of the poems, such as "Metamorphoses (A Russian fairy tale)," employ the spare and child-like simplicity and rhythms (as well as the slightly menacing undertones) of folklore or lullaby. Understatement and verbal economy heighten the elegiac resonance of poems such as "Requiem for a Dark Boy" ("Go, bitter polaris, go / gleam the green deep, / There a dark brother lies / mute and moist, / where all stars hide") and "For My Father" ("Not one drop of dry land, / beautiful old man / be in your dying"), which reflect on the deaths of the poet's brother, in a fishing accident, and her father, also a fisherman. "Overheard at the Oracle" presents perhaps the most radical movement in the direction of spare poetic lines and linguistic restraint, in nine sections revealing the influence of the traditional East Asian forms and content of the *I Ching*. The poems in the third, eponymously titled, section of *Silt of Iron* give evidence that a new style of writing is emerging, involving a more relaxed free verse line, a direct and unmediated engagement with history and present conditions, and a frequently ironic or directly emotional voice. This voice more often dares the blunt, prosaic statement and begins to shape a bravura persona, one who has "seduced, overthrown everybody" ("Stars and Foreign Bodies") and can acerbically declare of male posturing "Specious nonsense!" ("Definitive Lines on the Jewish-Slavonic Syndrome"). The sense of a living speaking voice, which begins to develop strongly here, will become characteristic of Fiamengo in her later work.

In Praise of Old Women (1976), published by Valley Editions, and *North of the Cold Star* (1978), by Mosaic Press, represent the maturation of this powerful and direct voice. Fiamengo has not renounced her earlier poetic preoccupations, for myth and fairy tale, as well as European history, remain important (particularly in poems about the relationship between women and power), but now the personal is no longer transmuted into archetype as in the earlier work. A bold "I" declares itself in many of the poems, a passionate, proclaiming self by turns tender, wry, or denunciatory. Frequently the poems of *In Praise of Old Women* address a particularized "you," the poem beginning as if in the middle of a conversation. As the title of this volume suggests, a number of the poems consider the plight of women, their roles in cultures ancient and modern; such women are at times vulnerable, maternal, nurturing, but also bold and vengeful. The angry title poem, with its insistent "I," use of contrasting images, and anaphoric lines for rhetorical power, represents Fiamengo's lucid declamatory style at its best: "and I tell you, Tadeusz, / I will grow old in America. / I will have no second debut. / I will raise my son on old battles, / Kosovo, Neretva, Thermopylae, / Stalingrad and Britain, / and I will wrinkle adamantly in America" ("In Praise of Old Women"). The other poems in the collection range widely in subject matter, from an intimate portrait of the poet's son as a teenager in rebellion against his mother, to a recollection of amputee veterans in Communist Yugoslavia, but in general this volume marks a turn by the poet to anchor her poems more firmly in her present time and place. Eastern Europe is present in allusion and contextual echoes, but the primary focus of the poet's eye is contemporary North American society and the landscapes of British Columbia.

The new poems published in *North of the Cold Star* further expand the range of this voice. Many are highly elegiac, considering the deaths of friends ("Requiem" and "Last Walk") and the fragility of all life and experience ("Point-No-Point" and "Atropos"); in addition, a new, more pointedly nationalistic and public register is achieved in poems such as "Acknowledge Him Canadian" and "To the R.C.M.P.: A Middle-Aged Lady's Plea." In poems such as these, Fiamengo expresses her deep love for Canada and her commitment to the ideals it might, with discipline and good faith, embody. While "Acknowledge Him Canadian" presents a majestic and idealized sweep of Canadian history and geography that unite in the person of one brave doctor, Norman Bethune, "To the R.C.M.P." recognizes, with a mixture of ironic chagrin and self-mocking hope, that the mythic portrait of the noble Mounted Police is not now, but might someday approach, reality.

Patience After Compline and *White Linen Remembered* present a deepening of the personal and introspective voice that developed in the previous volumes. In *Patience*, the elegiac tone is sounded frequently as the poet contemplates the long illness and death of her fierce mother and reflects on their difficult relationship. Yet bitter lament ("Faces Averted") and sorrowful recollection ("Prayer") are lightened by a complementary emphasis on religious wisdom and the gift of grace. This theme is frequently pursued, as in "Gradations of Grace," in poems of nature observation, where both the beauty and ceaseless flux of the poet's surroundings provide the occasion for spiritual insight, and the objects of the material world become "visible directives to the soul" ("The Oriole"). The questing of the earlier writing is here replaced by a wide faith and Biblically-inspired language and cadences "Nor does it know / as the white wind blows / from whence that frozen breathing / comes or where it goes" ("The Patience Tree"). In other poems, the poet's Slavic origins and reflections on Canadian culture are effectively counterpointed, with touches of feminist and nationalist humour to leaven the whole. Consolation is the keynote of *White Linen Remembered* and of the new poems that are presented here for the first time. Present and remembered grief is assuaged through poetry — "I comfort myself with singing" ("Vinka") — memories of the dead "in the hour / of vespers" ("Hobotnica") and a faith in "the possibles / of blessedness" ("Noctis Equi"). While these poems are imbued with an awareness of loss, they also celebrate the power of art to "rescue / the fading afternoon / from anonymity" ("Joseph Plaskett Sketching"). Poetry itself, "[t]he natural prayer / of the soul" ("Visible Living"), the contemplation of history, and the simple pleasures of "visible living" offer consolation for "the hard mysteries / of singularity" ("Singularity"). Caustic wit unsettles any too-easy certainties, as when we encounter the "agitated ants" in "Three Peonies."

The final poem in *White Linen Remembered*, "Circles and Painted Horses," sounds a note of farewell, as the speaker reflects on all those "[o]ld friends" who have left her to "ride soft / eyed into galactic distance"; but it also expresses the steadfastness of one who finds in nature's gifts the blessed promise of a "[d]esign to defeat / depredation." The poems themselves trace such a resonant design. These later works continue to draw on the language of liturgy. With its resonant simplicity of expression, the reflective voice meditates on the imagery of climate, location and landscape. Over more than five decades of memorable creative work, Marya Fiamengo has forged a unique European-nourished literary sensibility while remaining rooted in the singular reality and environment of British Columbia.

— Janice Fiamengo, Seymour
Mayne & Russell Thornton

from
THE QUALITY
OF HALVES
(1958)

The Quality of Halves

Into this dusk, a word whose vowel contains
The quality of halves,
Those slurred vibrations between the cheek
And palpitating wings of moths,
I hear half lost a voice
Along an edge of print that rims the mind.

And gyres begin to move
In the gray lower levels of the brain.
The heart sends up her red;
The eye strains out its pain for lapis lazuli,
That longing for the last intensity of blue.
In the ear the sound of water moves
And calls the aural shadow of the sail,
Dim and pale, a hum
Of Byzantium.

I had an Icon once when I was young.
I swallowed it
To be companion to my heart:
I hear it murmuring now,
A portent in the blood.
The Icon murmurs of Byzantium.

Out of the moths and darkness and *Dämmerung*-time
And the thick slow feeling when the veins
Multipy and drain the saltness from the blood
Leaving the marshes sweet about the tongue,
The sea sings to the clear blue levels of the mind.
Lapis lazuli is a window etched into the sky;
Icon and eye flutter the sail
To the gate in the circular wall:
Yeats on the rim of print,
Byzantium a port of call.

As Birds in their Mute Perishability

Because they are old we cherish them,
For what we were and are and are to be
Is now the tissue of their being.

My friends I can no longer hear upon the beach,
Their voices come like cavern sounds,
A liquid whorl of lostness as when ducks
Make suctions when they seek the sea,
And nothing young is seen
Except the leaf upon the tree, the loons
                in their seasonal waterings.

I am left to dream my starfish to the wood,
My tree upon the sea,
To cherish with my wrists the bones that will be old,
The bones of my paternity.

Dead wood and wanting of the flesh
And this caress of pebbles on the shore
Waiting the moist embracing of the sea,
Not these nor any sweep of heart
Can plead the leaf back to the pulseless tree
Nor wake the voiceless bird asleep
                in her mute perishability.

Only the funnel of the heart keeps
While yet the pulse beats
That voicelessness complete
When walking in the street:
You feel the wood and hear the loon
                and see the winter welcoming.

St. Alban's Revisited

Elegiac the mood of the winter water
brooded over the swans' white serenity
in a flow of snow movement
with snow crystals melting on a fold of wing,
disturbing nothing, only blending
whiteness with whiteness,
dampening the blanched river's frost shoreline,

the bells of the abbey clappering,
ringing out icicle petals of sound,
carillons of cold caught in the wreath of breathing.

In summer revisited
in the grown heat glow of August,
great in the fullness of trees,
green under the ripe serene blue of the meridian sky,
catching the identical swan postures
left over images of a winter's vision,
gliding like ineffable drops of silence,
a wing span of quiet on a murk of water,

bells brooding stillness in the abbey tower
holding a granary of sound suspended,
warm peace attends the fall of noon.

At the Lake

Oh take away the colours of the bright meridian day,
there is such a calling in my blood for gray,
for the mute moot mists that wait
watchful along the sedges of the lake.

I knew too late
the marshes were my home,
my dream to hide in fen and brake,
encrust myself in thick leaved trees
and while each limb moved slow
let my mind like the birds be lateral,
moving incanted from shore to shore.

If you opened out the oyster of my soul
her pearl would be gray.
There was a painter whom I knew
who praised the world in that hue;
his gray was luscent, mine's subdued.

Where do you go
bereft of that pastel repose —
to mountains which make
a barrier of space and take
the intense vibrations of the sun and sea,
wind them tight
in the dark green of conifers or the hard whites
of rocks without bracken
or the lichen
of my caressed inland water beds?

No, the heart
which sees the winter which it dreams
glint in the eye of a bird
flutters and falls apart,
dissolved in longing for
that sere deciduous shore
whose trees shed leaves like
feathers molting from the owls of desire.

Gladly I'll give up
the jewels in the caves, the eagles of the north,
to live in mist,
to walk in meditative sloth
as some Chinese in a heron-haunted print,
drowned in gray and soothed by the sere serene
marshes, the landscape of the only quiet
that I know.

Poem for Sarajevo

As some may dream of proud imprisoned queens,
precarious in the royalty of captive states,
and make of them their emblem-flower of liberty,
loving them fiercely in the large loyalty of dreams —
I dreamt of you and knew you instantly
a queen and mistress of mountain water,
all hallow-harrowed in your history, age-rich,
rich like that moment in the climbing morning,
when harvest-redolent the ripe tobacco
                    glints yellow armour
in a summer's tournament of field.
My green-gone-golden city, Sarajevo, hill-born,
making a slope of minarets and poplar trees,
the round and pointed diadem for your feast-day crown
when, pregnant from their icon-dark,
gaunt Byzantine saints, great with eyes,
stare hungry halos at the skies
where spiral the alienating cries
                    of the muezzin's call.

Caliph and vizier, now insubstantial,
                    leave shadows made tangible —
shadows on monuments, ghosts on hard rock,
                    phantoms in the bazaar,
brief reincarnations in the pointed slippers,
patient outside the yasmin door —
a debris mosaic of sadness and splendour.

And where and what was I who then was feasting with
                    an eye made wide with gladness,
with a heart gone celebrant and melting in my blood,
                    a mind drowning in the well of time?

For there in that hall of mountains I could hear
the murmurous, brothering destiny of the flesh that
                         clothes my bones
and I, no longer I, but all my mothering fathering tribe
beat instant with the pulse, was water with the voicing
                                        flood
which throbbed and flowed incessant circles around my
                                        being

as if, caught in some wood of nightingales,
I lengthened out my longing like a forest thinking backward
to the first ritual word in the liturgy of language,
spiralling into music like the smoke of incense
held forever in that residue of poignance —
the large-eyed icon yearning for its saint.

With the soft hands of your cathedral's dark,
orthodox, you placed a crown of candles on my heart
and now that beat illumines all my blood
and I in you, as you in me,
cathedral, mosque and bloody bridge,
will blaze in a flame of cherishing,
adding brightness to both our dusts.

The Logician, His System

You have a quick cerebral heart,
its beat more precise than mine;
it rhymes
with more important things than time.

And palsy,
palsy of the brain,
has never been your nightmare
nor the lame
your connoisseurs of friendship,
nor languages
you can't explain
your keys to everlastingness.

But I,
who move in slow moon-circles,
tidal, sea-river bred
will die
and never once accelerate my heart
to beat with you
in those auricle non-oracular heads.

The loons will cry
their winter dialectics for the dead
which you will hear
and print another page of dialogue
and be led across it with your eyes,
a pair of intellectual cohorts,
spies
to that cerebral celibating pulse,
the heart-in-head.

Epithalamium

We are not cold who live by myths,
wrapped in our dreams of love and fealty,
nor old as marble is in monument,
nor mindless like bald stones in crumbling battlement.

Not old, nor cold, nor carefully impervious,
but palpable, we breathe our breath of mist
to mute the harshness of impermanence
like moths who live between the candle and the wick
in a glimmer world of guttering and light;
yet our shadows are the chandeliers
whose kindling brings the heart alive.

Not old, nor cold, nor blazing meteorite,
but more the kith of nebulae
shaped in the dust of space and caused
by the dislocation of a star,
we are the votary people, the replenishers of night.

And I of all most bound in myth, most found in wish,
I offer you as one akin, the royalty of night:
we have the day for tedium.
Oh do not live republican and sane,
ruled by the day into a citizenry of small change,
but share this courtly exile of the night
and be imperial with the dark.

Were I occult and gracious with power,
regal in magic as well as intent,
I'd offer dominions to carry your names,
dispatch you an empire to shatter oblivion
and blazon amulets to cherish your fame;
mindful of fragrance, give myrrh for your pleasure,
jacinth to jewel your radiance of years
and sew with the fine twine of witchcraft
your bones and your sinews into enchantment
to last out felicity forever and a day.

With this alchemy turn the daytime
into a peacock's spreading tail,
no more republican but like the night
a sovereign of promise princely eyed
to charm every hurting harm away.

For we are not old, nor cold, nor self-bemused
who live by myths, who dance between the candle and the wick,
but warm and quick, the pulse behind the wrist,
the substance of the insubstantial breath.

Then take this dubious blessing from a wedding guest
who wishes you joy in your mortality,
to fashion poignancies sufficient for the heart
to cast her aura on eternity.

from

SILT OF IRON

(1971)

Metamorphoses

A Russian fairy tale

In the forests of Russia
that interior Russia
whose geography stretches
and touches my throat

In this interior Russia
a lizard sits dreaming
enchanted by zero
diverted by sloth
In the deep of the forests
of Russia
where bears dance
in the snow
where in the silence
of sunshine
rocks bloom
with lizards
asleep in the winter's
spare warmth

Should you stand
in that silence
and look at that lizard
you will see
on her head a small crown
and the skin of the lizard
will glitter
until the eye transfigures
the copper-green limbs
into a golden woman
upon a green throne

But Russia, my Russia of quiet,
my Russia of calm cold
the barbarians have come
for breakfast
the green throne and the golden woman
have gone and in the forest
the noise of the comfortable rabble
competes with the gabbling of gnomes

Our Ikon-Measured Walks

I often speculate on countries where they sleep
Behind green shutters on cool dappled beds
Lullabyed between the sheets
By the gratuitous dronings of the sea
And the gabble of cobbles in the street,

Where even my constant adversary
The harsh centurion sun,
Blazing with Roman purpose in the sky
Becomes a drowsy poppy, soporifically benign,
While I am for a moment tenderly resigned.

It's then the horns of puritan purpose blow,
But what they do not know,
My dear Oblomov, is that you and I
Are cousins and we love to lie
Continuously on sofas,

Making the cracked plaster walls grow wide
As a chasm-startled sky,
Those unfortunate marriages we made
Each with our pale puritan shade
Contributed little to this disease
And only robbed us of our splendid ease.

Neither the cold agitators of that other north
Who never understood our mouths
But urged a constant going forth
Nor the dedicated sensualists of the south
Praying for pleasure on the palazzo floor,

Brought up in mist and mountain snow
Implacable with the passion to define
We lie upon our sofas
Occasionally we sigh
For the clarity of the Mediterranean mind.

In vain as long as we can talk
We live in fortresses of sloth
And make occasion of our Ikon-measured walks,
Princely with words and pleased
While attendant trees

Spread canopies of thought to tease
Our murky skulls to further speech
Oh sofa-saturated cousin mine
What impervious virtue we make of killing time!

Yet dear Kin I love you more
Than any bright-eyed glad seignor
For both of us can look past Rome
Somnolently Byzantine
Bedded and bold
As mimosa blooming in the northern cold.

Requiem for a Dark Boy

Go, bitter polaris, go
gleam the green deep.
There a dark brother lies
mute and moist,
where all stars hide.

Go, glint a glow
where phosphorus, pale as snow
flints on that dark boy's brow.
Not skeletal yet,
that flesh is wet.

He lies where coral's sown,
where polyps roam.
Full fathom five
means not alive.

Pole star, bold star,
cold as the dark boy's bones
stare through the smirk of foam.
Tell him through bubbles,
the bauble is broken,
vessel empty,
no body home.

For My Father

I

An old man
            on a white sheet
fluttering
            in your cage of bones
wounded
            tremulous pulse
with your time
            wound down.

Good-bye
            dear man.
I should
            have brought you
the Sea
            in a pail
but instead
            I brought you
my grief —
            it was salt.

II

Personal and private
is an old man's dying.
He lies spent —
foam on the sand,
shallow ebb
where barnacles edge.

Then sea be his element
Salt the taste he loved
carry bone and blood
to final ocean bed.

Water bless
all of him,
hands, heart, and head.
Not one drop of dry land,
beautiful old man
be in your dying.

The Bamboos

This winter the snow
and bitter wind
almost destroyed
the thin tenacious stalks
of the bamboo plants
in the garden.

I went out to save them.
The wind was blowing
north-north-east.
I felt the storm's
cutting sleet
clean to the marrow
of my bones.

Fingers numb
face wet with snow,
I struggled with string,
stalk and burlap sacking.

∞

The wind has died down,
the snow gone,
the plant strong but bent
survived.

Yesterday someone unexpected
came, tidied the disorders
of the garden.
The bamboos stand straight
in proud vegetative grace.

Old cruelties reprieved
linger in the green
of its new leaves.

Overheard at the Oracle

Nine Poems of Chance Based on the I Ching,
The Chinese Book of Changes

1

ONE FOR THE HEXAGRAMS

The dragon flies in the heavens
The mare walks upon earth
Heaven and earth do not meet
Except at the extremities.

2

ONE FOR THE TRIGRAMS

The moon is nearly at the full,
A heron calls in the reeds.
I have replenished the goblet,
I will share it with you.
The heron calls
Its young answer.
This is the affection of
        the inmost heart.

3

ONE FOR THE DARK LINES

Water over the lake

Things cannot be forever separate:
Heaven and earth have their
                   limitations
Thus the four seasons of the year
                 arise
It furthers one to create
            number and measure

To set limits even to the waters
of the lake.

4

ONE FOR THE BRIGHT LINES

In the symbolic sequence of the Later Heaven
The earth stands in the southwest.
Thunder and Rain set in:
Heaven and Earth deliver themselves,
The seedpods of all growing things
Break open,
The image of Deliverance
Spans the sky.

5

ONE FOR THE YIELDING

Lakes resting one on the other
The image of the joyous
What is not weighed
Is at peace
Possesses inner truth
Even pigs and fishes
Share in this good fortune.

6

ONE FOR THE UNYIELDING

The escape of the soul
Brings about change.
Return to the beginning
And pursue to the end,
Thus can be known
The condition of the outgoing
And returning spirit.
Satisfaction with this knowledge
Leads to the practice of love.

7

ONE FOR THE YIN

The prince shoots at the hawk
On a high wall
The courtier kills three foxes
In the field
And receives a yellow arrow.
The ablution has been made
But not yet the offering.
The great depart, the small approach.
It furthers one to exert those influences
Which lead to the contemplation
Of the light of the kingdom.

8

ONE FOR THE YANG

A wild goose gradually draws near the shore.
A crane calls it to the shade.
Ten pairs of tortoises cannot oppose them.
They have come to share the generous goblet
Which the woman offers.
The oxen have halted.
The man's hair and nose being cut off
He rolls his eyes,
The wagon wheels are broken,
The spokes fly asunder.
Not a good beginning
But at the lake shore
A good end.

THE LAST FOR THE IMMUTABLE PRINCIPLE CHANGE, THE RULER OF THE UNIVERSE

This is the perfection of steadfastness,
That its beauty is within.
The colour of the earth is yellow.
The blood of the dragon black.
These must not compete.
They are the complements of courage.
Therefore not outward adornment
But dwelling in essentials
Gives freedom to the limbs
Song its expression.

Stars and Foreign Bodies

I only want to rest
in the midst of your arms.
For this I would give up
the imperious authority of my eyes
which have brought down stars
and foreign bodies in their time.

Yet you evade me.
I who have subdued,
seduced, overthrown everybody:
seedy British novelists,
policemen and Polish poets,
Chinese diplomats, dull Academics,
Insurance Agents and tight-lipped
men from the Russian Embassy.

Only you resist me successfully.
I don't want your soul
or your china and fine linen.
Save those for God or the government
or your wife.

But please reconsider.
Because I only want
the temporary splendour of your hair,
and your arms around me late,
late at night.

The High Cost of Eternity

Eternity was in our lips and eyes,
but you must have misunderstood
the message
and raced home to mortality.

I understand you live underground
in a crystal palace
surrounded by quartz and stalagmites.
That also is one kind of durability.

But the message spoke of eternity,
and I think bliss was mentioned
and heaven but not home.

Home is where one pays the bills.
Faces debts and debtors.
Heaven is all arrears,
the amplitude of living beyond one's means.

But then not all of us
are given to immortal longings.
And the cost of losing Empires
of any kind
is always high.

Golden These Children

Golden these children,
their eyes devouring bright
lit by the fires of fixed androgynous minds.
You may think it simple to resist
the shrill pubescent clamor of their lips.

The twist, my friends, is this.
They pay one hommage of a kind,
are quick to remind that divinity
like Ariadne left behind
by manly Theseus on a rock
near Crete, divinity
must pay its founding price.

Maternal in shape
it seems my fate
to carry boyhood
always in my arms.
No one comes cruelly close
who does not ask comfort for his harm.

And those who chose
difficult Dionysus for their thighs
must rock
a cosmic cradle in-between
the baby talk.

Definitive Lines on the Jewish-Slavonic Syndrome

for Miriam Waddington

My dear,
Do not, even in the Siberian exile of the wasted self,
call those paltry men who loved and left you noble.
For I have a dossier on them,
written in their own crooked liturgy and language.
And I have read it all,
read it in its original hypothetical but primitive
Old Germanic.

It is not the "noble ethic of renunciation"
as they like to call it.
Nor what is known in Anglo-Saxon
as the "noble ethic of endurance."
It is only self-absorbing prudence,
a cautious bandage
left over from the Jutland Marshes.

Gospoja,
poets come
and poets go in every language.
Lermontov wrote,
"I am not Byron
but another
I suffer more
my soul is Russian."

Specious nonsense!
It only comes to this
that some of us have learnt to suffer
more loudly than others.
The pain is always the same.

But we
who keep a salon in the ghetto
know the blushing Aryan boys
who only want a mildly rapturous blood transfusion
for the antiseptics running in their veins.

You must be certain, lady,
to distinguish these
from wilful Antony, indiscreet;
or brilliantly diseased Byron
dying of fever
for Greece.

Baba Yaga

We met at high noon
there was no sun,
the weather typical of our country
was damply grey.

Somewhere in the back of my heart
I heard the rattle of Turkish sabres
and the chill fact of Kosovo
ran down my back.

Your eyes were darker
and blacker than mine
and you laughed a great deal
abruptly
like a dog barking at the moon.

I did not like you,
although we once shared a common enemy,
and you paraded a common love.
I knew you for what you were
the Armenian Baba Yaga
of all my Russian nightmares,
the hag who chews up children
with teeth of iron
or the witless gnome
in the music of Mussorgski.

Madam, I give you your due
and your measure,
the purlieus of waste.
May your soul sit forever
in stale cafes
where the odour of grease
will finger the shapeless
squalor of your hair.

Because of you
and your pedlar's pack of pleasure
something bravely arterial and splendid
bleeds dimly though my severed veins
and dies.

Zagreb

Bougainvillaea —
bougainvillaea breathing in the street
using up the rancid air
leaving fragrance in its place.

Bougainvillaea
followed by the smell of garlic
like a peasant courtship
clumsy in the side lanes,

sound of kitchen dialects
slurred in the halls
of old Croatian houses
homely palaces, Jelacic,
in the street of Stjepan Radic.

Croatia:
a language and a people
running barefoot in the streets of Zagreb.
Follow!
Follow all the syllables of longing
names and places —
the ZAGREBASKO GORE,
Square of the Victims of Fascism,
the wooden stairs of TOMICEVA Street
GRIC,
again the square, named for the heroes
                    of the revolution,
square with the tiled church roof
stained in the implacable colours of resistance.

Zagreb, fortress,
city built for straw-haired, flat-faced
                              stubborn peasants,

I walked there
bougainvillaea in my nostrils
on my tongue the dust-mote moths of history
palpitating like machine gun bullets.
PREKREZJE, the chestnut trees
mix their odour with stale urine, spoiled olive oil
                              ubiquitous onion,
smells communal and private
co-existant.

Zagreb,
hill fort
eminence of the SAVA,
that hometown river which flows
through arteries and channels
empties in my heart
a silt of iron.

For Osip Mandelstam

A "proletariat of petals and bullets,"
presses against my chest.
Breathing is difficult.
I am cold.
I cannot live in such a small
         corner of the flesh.
The radar of defeat
like the Star of David
glints on my wrist.

Can you comfort me
Pablo Neruda
for Osip Emilyevich Mandelstam,
a bag of brittle Jewish bones
broken in Siberia.

The white bleached snow
         of Vorkuta
eats at my eyes.
And you impeccable Michael Sholokoff
lend me your Cossacks' rose coloured
         sun glasses
because I am blinded by
a collective necessity
which would intern the sun.

Remorseless, implaccable destiny
where pogroms fall through the air
like programmes at a Sunday concert,
I would give up everything
especially history
for mercy and justice,
a little tender sanity.

If at the end of the pain,
the blessing;
and clear in the midnight frost
above the walls of the Kremlin
sparkles the dark standard
of the Virgin of Kazan;
even a sulphur match might
keep me warm and alive.

from
IN PRAISE OF
OLD WOMEN
(1976)

Winter's Tale

Beside her bed but out of sight
She kept the fairy stories
            of her native land.
Some day she thought
Some day in Autumn
            when the weather
Is quite right,
Ripe but not hot
I'll go.

For in her heart
She wanted to be Queen
Although she kept the purpose
                  dark
And to that end
She plotted fierce assassinations
            in her mind,
Murdered common places
One at a foul time.

Occasionally she went to gaol.
Here she read the stories over
Found that in tale after tale
The queens were old or cruel
The princesses honey young
With gems in their eyes
And jewels like plums of pleasure
            on their tongues.

Steadfast she reminded
Her desire reaffirmed.
She wanted to be Queen
Albeit she recognized
　　　　　the apple in the worm.
Whether cold, or old, or mean.
She wanted to be Queen.
Queens were forever
Princesses were not real.

This you see
Was all the shelter
　　　　she could seize;
Knowing princesses, no matter
　　　　how they please
Princesses, are not forever.
Only Queens are real.

Fat in Fairyland

Always to be fat in fairyland!
What an affliction.
Seldom in real life
do I meet a fat fairy.

But oh, in Paradise
there is God,
there are Cherubim
          and Seraphim
Virtues, Dominions, Powers.
Surely one of these is fat.

Overheard at the Pornographer's

"Men over forty are attractive
women are merely middle-aged."

Mortality, my friend
is not confined to women over forty,
much as you might wish it.

Incarcerate yourself
before   behind
beside   inside
the nubile flesh
of pretty girls,
strut that spurious virility
as you must
despise the wrinkled female face
the heavy breasts
the sprouting veins
that grim pimp
will have his price.

And copulation
in the brightest light
will not reprieve
the temporary silver
in your hair
caught like the sea
between the storms
of fretful vanity.

I call on all the awesome
women of the night
the temple proud tall
women of the past
Hecate, Medea, and great Artemis
to salt that shrinking parcel
of protruding limb
into petrified eternity.

Born on the wind of anger
drops of fire sing
in the arterial breath
of the years to come.
You will be beggared yet
who cannot love
except increase of self
in some pubescent child's face.

Growth

So many green and growing years
an albatross of trust and need
you fondled at my neck
crept out of nightmare sheets
into my cranky bed of sleep.

Now stubborn tall, gawky brash
you hang a single sign upon your door.
Knock!

While on your face
dotted like acne
the letters
noli me tangere are writ bold.

Autumn in Osoyoos

Apples
yellow   apples
harvest   mandalas
halos in green boughed trees.

Sulk   of   sulphur
smudge   of   mustard
in the cottonwood trees.

Along the road
a dark full woman
with her oat blond daughter
carries tomatoes.

They are Greek or Portuguese
redolent each
of ripe Demeter
and young Persephone.

Mice

Everybody's
      implacable mouse
eats at the bread of life.
With some
he is polite
and takes only small bites.

Signs of the Times

Conifer   green
glacier   blue
Nelson   city
a crystal
polished   clean
by the patina
of quiet   July heat
in the summer of 1973

the sign
in the arboreal bus
driving though hilltop streets
into the hemlock hearts
of Kootenay trees
the sign,   benign,
reads,

"Be kind to animals
they have feelings,   too."

In July of 1954
on a mended trolley
with broken   wooden seats
in the city of Zagreb
men with amputated limbs
leant against   a   sign
which said; in blanched white letters
on dried red,

"Only wounded heroes of the Revolution
and pregnant women
may sit."

Elegy for Ann

Two candles burning
at St. André Avelin
a woman dying
in Victoria.

The question raw
as seagull's cry
why, lady, why
drift into ebb
of final tide?

I thought to tie
your vital breath
with ropes of prayer,
moor the quick pulse
to rocks of hope.

Reluctant to forgo
the rituals of faith
ceremonies of trust
that fail to stay
the course of falling stars.

At sea's far edge
she slips to ocean bed.
There, lady, rest.
Freighted with friends
anchored by progeny
your name a testament
to grace.

Ann, now calm
as sand
tide leads you
and leaves you
Pacific.

Orthodox Easter

In memory of A.M. Klein

Candles, eggs and Easter bread
upon the table white are laid.
The Ikons in the holy house proclaim
that Christ is risen,
our Christ is risen, once again.

The anthems rise
the liturgy ascends
ecstatic voices sing transcendent praise
intoxicated lungs incensed with ritual
brave proclaim
a trust for life
beyond transfixing wood
immuring stone,
in love with love of flesh
transfigured into bone.

Three times the holy kiss
is given people, book, and priest.
Three times they kiss
denying Peter thrice,
the pride of people proud
who sing the glory of the angel
Byzantine.

Bowing to the Ikons on the wall,
Oh Ikon, Ikon, grave and tall
whose is the fairest faith of all?
For pierced upon the golden tree
a humbled thin-faced ghost I see
blessing old souls in ghetto lanes for me.

In Praise of Old Women

Yes, Tadeusz Rozewicz, I too
prefer old women.
They bend over graves
with flowers,
they wash the limbs of the dead,
they count the beads of their rosaries,
they commit no murders
they give advice
or tell fortunes,
they endure.

In Poland, in Russia,
in Asia, in the Balkans,
I see them shawled, kerchiefed
bent-backed, work-wrinkled.

But Tadeusz,
have you been to America?
Where we have no old women.
No Stara Babas,
no haggard Madonnas.

Everyone, Tadeusz, is young in America.
Especially the women
with coifed blue hair
which gleams like the steel
of jets in the daytime sky.
Smooth-skinned at sixty,
second debuts at fifty
renascent
they never grow old in America.

And we have in America
literate, sexually liberated women
who wouldn't touch a corpse,
who confuse lechery with love,
not out of viciousness
but boringly
out of confusion, neurosis, identity-crises.

Tadeusz,
I go to the cemetery
with my mother
one of us stoically old,
the other aging,
and I tell you, Tadeusz,
I will grow old in America.
I will have no second debut.
I will raise my son on old battles,
Kosovo, Neretva, Thermopylae,
Stalingrad and Britain,
and I will wrinkle adamantly in America.

I will put salt in the soup
and I will offer bread and wine
to my friends,
and I will stubbornly praise old women
until their thin taut skins
glow like Ikons ascending on escalators
like Buddhas descending in subways,
and I will liberate all women
to be old in America
because the highest manifestation of wisdom,
Hagia Sophia,
is old and a woman.

from

NORTH OF THE

COLD STAR

(1978)

Acknowledge Him Canadian

Know these for Canadians.
They walk muffled into history
muffled by snow and loyalty
Geography their native destiny.

Acknowledge them Canadian.
Intransigent lovers of fur
     and wilderness
     Indian women
     portages — canoes.

Recognize them ancestral voyageurs
     Army   Chaplains
     Bishops   Bankers
     Whitemen   Redmen
Pinched by love of a cold climate
into fleur-de-lys purple and Tory blue.

These bred us Canadian
     stoic as granite
     persistent as glaciers
     baffled by snowdrifts
     bemused by flakes
into a craze for the far boundaries of northern lakes.

Led us land claimants
lovers of landscape
gave us *coureur-de-bois* literature
western liturgies
names like landlocked litanies
of lake and river
mountain pass and garrisoned stockade.

Praise them as prodigal
spare men made passionate
by distance and terrain.
Call them Canadian

     Deguire   Waddin
     Henry   Mackenzie
     Thompson   Bethune.

Out of this storehouse
    of bone and blood
out of river and mountain and marsh
Came one man
from many men
some noble minded
some cold with greed
the addicts of steel.

But more of them
lean men
devotees of insistent virtue
inheritors of minor nobilities

True to the cold star
    the pole star
    the north land.

Beyond Lake Superior limestone
beyond prairie intractability
beyond Pacific plenty
out of the nation's marrow
    and sinew

Came one man
a white star
a man of moral integrity
no pillar of state, church
            or society
Yet a descendant of all these.

Our best self
gathered into a single cell.
A man noble-minded
of value to the people

This man came
like a meteor out of Ontario
into the red dawn of China
a man of value to us
and to all people.

Know him as Norman Bethune.
Acknowledge him Canadian.

Requiem

for Pat Lowther

Earth and salt water
bless and absolve
the burning of this flesh
which walked the hard road
of genesis.

Noble-minded peace
bequeath this breast bereaved of breath
graced by language
quit of time
enduring innocence.

Quick that spirit
proud that hair
brave the hands
which played the music
those words made.

All her mortal bones
undressed
sing to us now
through caves of space
requiescat lady, rest
your white heart
burns clean and live
as hottest star
or farthest nebulae.

October 24, 1975

Last Walk

A last walk
by the long lake.
I think of you
in surgical white —
pray for healing.

Will you heal
in harvest autumn,
winter already
zero in your bone?

The road a grey
dust of frayed ribbon
framed by the lake's
unrelenting blue.

The willows alive
green as wishes
I grieve for you.

Point-No-Point

Sitting at the table
very old
thin grey hair
braided —
wound about the head —
a coronet
celebrating longevity

Beyond —
The Strait,
Juan de Fuca
gleams
like a polished Spanish knife

Salal leaves
In copper jugs
blue and white
china cups

The old woman
cuts the stems
of green grapes
with silver scissors
we drink tea
pour cream
from pewter
eat cinnamon buns

On the wall
steel engravings
a Tudor woman
face very plain
antique furniture
richly inlaid

The cinnamon buns
toasted russet brown
the same rich shade
as the folds
of the Tudor gown

The eye moves
past the patina
of furniture
to the patina
of God

The old woman
rubbed clean
clear as grace
the burnished sea
beyond the great
greening foliage
of island trees
arbutus cedar
scrub oak

Green grapes
green trees
salal
tenacious
faltering hands
offering tea and cakes
pushing back death
and wilderness.

Santa Cruz Revisited

All about
the city of the holy cross
hardwood eucalyptus
grows.

In granite bowls
small junkos bathe
California quail
perch delicate
frail as faith
on the patio rail.

A horseman rides
on a distant hill
his white horse poised
in a mustard field.

Along the road
the camelias bleed,
ice plants lick
at garden rocks
with thick
pink tongues.

In the streets
of Santa Cruz
a craze
of yesterday's rock
music plays away
the derelict days
of flower children
gone to grey seed.

Across the valley
from Aptos
on Meder Street
the cemetery gates
are locked.

The Jewish dead
sleep
piously wrapped
in the prayer shawls
of mortality.

Above
in the momentarily
neutral sky
no hawk flies.

Atropos

No longer young
yet not quite old
I feel the tides of death
pull at my veins

I sit among
calm weather men.
They are kind
as only those are kind
on whom the gods
have laid eccentric hands.

But I am not resigned
I want to die
on some far frontier
of an unrelinquished mind.

I close my eyes
and think about
my clear voiced aunt
old and gaunt
but piercing in her glance
dressed in black
a distaff in her hand
fateful as Atropos.

The talk goes on.
We speak of bishops
and of kings
on the patio rail
sit three sombre quail
dressed in the plummage
           of passage.

In another climate
under different stars
my aunt has died.
She was a Sibyl
to a simple people
living near the sea.
She blessed me once.

I grieve for her,
for she was queenly,
queenly as ripened wheat
not rich, but sovereign
of her kind,
she nourished life
and knew the cost
of progeny.

I sit.
The talk recedes.
The quail take flight.
My face is pale,
pale for my kin and gender.

To the R.C.M.P. —
A Middle-Aged Lady's Plea

Liberal anarchists
may sneeze
but I am usually
pleased
with the Royal Canadian Mounted Police.

In the scarlet and gold
of dress parade
I see them bold
as Byzantine angels
as they gingerly hold
rather flat
but certainly shining swords.

Yes, I know
power politics may
perforce
cause them on occasion
to consort
with the C.I.A.
or reluctantly
pick the locks
of the presumed
F.L.Q.

But surely
such mild misdemeanors
on the part of
Byzantine angels
are small potatoes.

Still, I would plead
doux, R.C.M.P.
remember the noblesse oblige
inherent in being
this Dominion's
only neo-platonic
police.

Make duplicate keys
to heaven
and leave
burglary to dead politicians
like Charles de Gaulle
who misconceived
identities
or C.D. Howe's
Yankee expertise.

Because we
R.C.M.P.
don't pretend
to be
the sweet home
of liberty.

We only
stand on guard
for the true
and the strong
and, of course,
the North
because like
our winter rivers
we know
that in certain
blessed seasons
we flow
free.

So may I
gently remind,
toute le monde,
that the price of being
both Neo-platonic
and Byzantine
is eternal
internal integrity.

from

PATIENCE AFTER

COMPLINE

(1989)

Gradations of Grace

Outside birds fly
serene in their order

The white iris nods
at the forthright rose

And patience I am told
obtains everything

The bloom and finish
of the peony, the gold

Of the laburnum, desire
for sea ebb and flow

Serene in their order
the stones warm under the sun

The purple of the lilac proclaims
the casual poise of primogeniture

The stir and storm of growth
sheen of the first born

The rock sits the grass grows
rain falls into the wind

White moths flutter and pause
above the green lichen

Slow as the seepage of sleep
this order blends faith
into gradations of grace.

The Voice of Matter

The rain falls
        drop beats on drop
        all things are as water.
Flood, flux, flowing
soft soft the voice of water
        fluid whispers
What except God is constant?

Not the deities of creek or stream
        not wind
                not weather
Not praise, nor love, nor language.

Silence perhaps and the music
        of movement
the blue space between pine boughs
the white light which cuts
        like a sword
in the truth of the morning.

The Oriole

Like distant and improbable happiness
the oriole flashes across my eye
to sit in the willow grove.

There it sings of green
orange brilliant, imperial.

I plod my way home
through a memory of oriole
summer haze of butterflies
weightless as symbols of blessedness
visible directives to the soul.

The Patience Tree

Under the bent green tree
I sit to dream
It is my own
this crippled aged tree.

The gardener pleads,
remove the tree
see the dry leaves
how they curl
in comfortless disease.

But I say
it is an olden
patient tree
in every spring
it comfort brings.

In autumn ripeness
blemished fruit
from knotted branch
falls heavily.

Along its base
the ivy creeps.
In a winter's grief
chill arms reach
my bird cage heart
in broken speech.

And the round-eyed moon
moves through the deep
black of startled stems
blessed with light
as the poet blest
the orient rich immortal
                    wheat.

Nor does it know
as the white wind blows
from whence that frozen breathing
comes or where it goes.

Blown bare of leaves
the spare boughs raised
speak silent praise
praise silence endlessly.

Faces Averted

If I could order
a fleet of taxis
place you central
in the cavalcade

I would escort you
in an entourage
past all the deficient signposts
of our lives.

And what would it prove?

That we sit together
hands not touching
faces averted
cross-grained and at odds
with one another

That raised voices
were our constant salute
not bitter but involuntary
like the raised fists
of an oppressed people

Longing for justice
but willing to settle
            for kindness.

Prayer

Rest it is nothing mother
rest it is everything
everywhere.   Sleep
you could never sleep.

Rest do not live
ferocious in the moment.   Let
the sweet air dissolve
this blight.   Drop the burden
which I carry.

It is summer. The sun
stuns us both with its magnificence.
Turn your head toward
the pristine scent of grass.

Oppressed pulse pause
resist the injured
watch of the tick-tock
clock. See where water
lies flat on the far field
flows toward horizon's edge.

Cease, oh clapperless bell.
Release.

Light in the Garden

I want to remember you
in the garden.   Bending over
the flowering garlic gathering
leek and opulent onion.

Once you were solid as salal
staunchly unbroken.   Something
of Demeter in your devotion
to growth.

I want to remember you
in the garden. Placing tomatoes
our vivid trophies into a chipped
white bowl.

Rest in my mind
in the light of the garden.
Let the white air of summer
fill your lungs in the garden.

Once you were fragrant
green as parsley. Now
sere faded flora pressed
in a black book.

At Batoche

Below.   Deep.   Engorged
we hear the river flow.
See it, the stern aloof
the deliberate Saskatchewan
northern with power, elemental as fate.

In the black scent of poplars
an owl hoots.   Reverent we cross
the battlefield.   We have come,
three friends, poets in the primal
garden, to keep vigil.

The chill moonlight casts fatal
shadows on our tardy witness. It
is cold. Colder the white bones
beneath the black earth
at Batoche.

Bear and Apple Tree

Evening at the farm —
we about to leave —
I glance toward the hill
and the apple tree.

There snuffling
the clear blue air
is a young bear.

Intent on apples
poised for fruit
an animal of slow
winter sleep
patient he waits
for our retreat.

We watch him
move manorial
momentary beneath the tree
as we, farewell burdened
move into our machine.

Behind us
a small wind whistles
in the branches.
The engine whines, catches.

We drive the long curves
of the Squamish highway
into neon-lit darkness
toward the bland cushions of apartments,
the bare proposition of pavement to tree.

Qui Vive?

I loved them both
stalwart Montcalm
                    soldierly
on his black horse

Wolfe, delicate
                    irritable Wolfe
dead in a maze
            of flags.

The curfew tolls,
the day dies down.
I sit under the bloom
of the spring pear tree

Reading,
holding at bay
the persistent sibilants
of Mama's
Adriatic voice.

"Stop reading,
work on your embroidery,
no one of substance
will marry you."

Balkan vowels,
Balkan manners
                    thrown
into the back garden
like grenades,
fusillades of gunfire.

Qui vive?
I read
et a quel regiment?

De la reine

I close the books,
The Letters of Wolfe
Dominion of the North,
nod at the voice
from the porch.

No mama,
no one of substance
shall marry me.
Not Wolfe, not Montcalm.

Mais mama
Qui vive?
The paths of glory
lead us where?

To western separatism
and the P.Q.
where they think
on the whole, mama
not unlike you.

"Greatness lies in response
to the moment.
Clarify who you are
when you lived,"
rattles Lady Juliette
from *The Wars.*

My war with sober
      village banalities
my mother's war
      with poetry and poverty
Quebec's war with language.

Queens have died
young and fair.
Who is to say
forever and for each day
who of substance
will marry whom?

Dust has closed
more than Helen's eyes.
Snow falls.
The curfew calls
us home to final place.

Comely Mary

or Sunday Morning Snow, Toronto.

For me the wonder
    the snow-fall soft
    on the crisp pavement
    the Sabbath holy calm.

I from the damp
    alluvial sea wet
    of a western coast

See the sun
    slurred yet blessed
    in the blur
    of a winter sky

Take delight
    in the street names
    richly resonant of England:
        Yarmouth   Palmerston
        Manchester   Melville.

The harvest of face
and race richer:
Portuguese   Greek
Ukrainian   Korean.

At the street corner
    dressed in Ontario
    red brick Sunday best:
    the Korean Presbyterian Church.

I paused bemused
            into my mind intrudes
            comely Mary, Queen of Scots
            desperate Rizzio
            unforgiving John Knox.

And somewhere
like a nimbus
distance tossed
the Lord God Buddha

                                lost.

Lord and Stalin

Bold black on the white
                    van
the letters read
Lord and Stalin.

Promised in smaller
                    print,
upholstery and fine
                    craftsmanship.

Yes, fine the upholstery
          of the Lord
          the giver of Life
from whence the well springs
                    come on high.

Juxtaposed against
the force of steel,
the meticulous craft
of terror, torture, pain.

A lord of death, ˙
          non-giver of life,
          tyranny's meticulous artisan.
The workmanship careful:
          kulaks extinguished,
          confederates betrayed,
          a people destroyed.

The white van moves on.

I am left in a blur
          of snow and history
          chilled on an innocent
          Ontario street.

Le Troglodyte du Marais

The long billed wren
known in French
as *le troglodyte du marais*
is a dweller in caves.

In short is
a bird disposed
to nest in holes.

This troglodyte
of the marsh
may build as many
as nine decoy nests.

The false nests
on dit are built
by the male
of the species.

The true nest
built by the female
of the species
for reasons,
according to naturalists,
unknown

are abundantly clear
to any number
of women
I know.

Alive Alive Oh! — A Parable

for Leslie Armour

A Canadian dean
at an American university
once intervened
on behalf of an unstable physicist
who repeatedly taught
that electrons were alive.

This it seems
is heresy of a kind
for while Americans are especially
partial to matter they do not
necessarily like it alive.
Ample evidence suggests
they prefer it inert.

But our dean was a Canadian
who dreamt of a home
lit by northern lights
yearned for the tundra
longed for salmon slippery seas
and the Queen smiling
tentatively at René Levesque.

Therefore with commendable esprit
in the habitual practice
of impartial inquiry known
as a Royal Commission
this dean decreed
a course must be designed
in the cosmology of physics
where electrons might be allowed
in a mystic religious sense
to live as matter might be said
to aspire to grace.

The friendly foreign dean
eventually returned
to where electrons live forever
magnetic in the true north.

The unfortunate physicist
of the mystic eye
remained behind in the centre
of empire.

Volatile as fire
he declined
into an institution without degrees
only particles of strange design
where neither electrons nor mind
remain for long alive.

Ethnic Gender

To be ethnic
is not necessarily
                    exotic!

Chick peas
and lentils
are no substitute
                    for porridge.

As a child
I longed to wear
kilts
live with chintz
                        sofas
hear the soft buzz
of wasp voices
not the slavic rasp
of my mother's
                    mother tongue,
where even the verbs
have gender.

Waking in the morning
to hear the sawdust stove
                        rebuked
for its reluctance
to provide heat
every word
declined in the feminine
                            ending
and I
the only other
female in the house.

My implacable mother
more totalitarian than

                Stalin

calling me
an open wound
in her side

Me
acned
unfortunate
barely post-menstrual

              Me.

Stigmata
to maternity!

I longed
for restrained vowels
understated emotions.
I fell in love
with Winston Churchill
Boys Own Annual
      and cracked Wedgewood
forever.

Regarded rice pudding
          and tapioca
as haute cuisine
So please remember
when you pour cream
      on your porridge
one woman's menu
is some child's poison.

You can have excess
of cabbage rolls
baklava and strudel
I prefer habeas
        corpus.

Conversations with Hagia Sophia

or A Meditation on St. Valentine's Day
and The Quiring of the Young-Eyed Cherubim

From the first
it was clearly
the language
that touched me.

Those woodbirds who
            begin to woo
            that impulse
from the vernal wood
      chariots of fire, arrows of desire.

Those spelt ardour
            rapture, the luminous
            and transcendent promise
            of eternity on lips
            in eyes.

Now on the eve
            of certain days
I dial zero or ought
as the British say
as in ought to
or more sinister
ought not to.

In such matters
as domesticity
and/or rumpled sheets
largely: ought not to.

On reflection
it strikes me
that while others
discover orgasmic hedonism
I discovered old women.

This led
to a totalitarian state
of living alone and liking it.
Gloating over closets
shared with none
dedicated entirely
to the triumphant assertive

                    self.

Yet on certain
        solemn feasts
or bright occasions
as mentioned, I dial
zero to infinity.

When finally I connect,
and this is not assured,
I hear a hum, the distant
concord of sweet sound
for which I yearn.

The room, my squalid
ordinary bedroom
is diffused, dissolves
in amber light.
The telephone receiver glows,
the hum grows stronger.

It is, of course,
the young-eyed cherubim
        quiring!

I wait. The air grows
sweetly still. A clear
cool contralto breaks in.

Office of the highest manifestation
        of wisdom, Hagia Sophia
        speaking.

Ah, Sophia, you at last.
I need an incandescent
word or two of hope.

Sympathetic silence.
Then the dialogue follows:
I am very discouraged, Sophia.
So you always are.
But it is getting worse.

The spoils, the stratagems, the treason.
Who said it would not.
Help! Have you nothing
better to offer?

I told you once
I repeat again
I inspire, I exhort
I admonish, I suggest
I do not coerce, I do not execute.
If you want execution you have
        the wrong office.
Try the executive branch.

The executive branch
may I remind you
is not musical.
They consistently turn
the volume down.

They complain about
singing orbs, do not enjoy
the music of the spheres.
Are less than partial
to quiring. Who do you
think invented rock and roll
          and guns?

I know what you want:
rational civil discourse
on the international scale.
Chaucer's trouthe and honour
old fashioned courtesies.
Not hearts and flowers
          today
Nuclear holocaust
          tomorrow.

What can I say?
Keep trying!   *Nil desperandum*
and other clichés!

Remember, I am on your side,
and I am not entirely negligible
nor ineffectual, although
patriarchy has tried
to make me so.

I agree St. Valentine
deserved demotion.
Fixations on erotic
and romantic love
are dim.   Retarded.

They may however
point in the right direction

Concentrate on Fidelio
banish the pornographics
of the Marquis.

I must go.   The young-eyed
cherubim are beginning to sing
out of tune. They do if left
too long unattended.

Thanks for ringing.
Keep in touch.
Give that impulse from
        the vernal wood
another chance.

And yes, but rarely,
eternity does settle
on lips and eyes.
The point is not
to miss the message.

Raspoloženje

"I cannot live without history"
R.A.D. FORD

To live without history
is to nurture a fool's dream
of oblivion.   Follow a faithless
heraldry. Run after rain with
a sieve. Escape into deserts of stone.

Apples catch fire and frost
glitters on the rowan berries. The river
frets and the tides retreat. What
holds us clear and luminous
in the present? Breathing? Devotion
to being? For answer the world
turns. Flowers seed under the earth.

On certain damp and mist-chill
days when the sky is wet Vancouver
grey, blank and featureless as fog,
I recall light in the square.

I remember courtesy.   August
in Sarajevo.   Partisan soldiers
who direct me to the museum of
state and history.   I witness patience
for halting accents, broken speech mended
in the hills of Bosnia.   Acknowledge
mountain freshness. The feel
of cold clean water. Observe
resemblances.   Kindred.   Topography
left behind in another climate.   Doukhobours
folded like linen handkerchiefs in the
pockets of Kootenay valleys.

II

It steals over me.   A mood
of the soul.   Raspoloženje.   I lean
on it like the lame lean on a strong
stock.   Bosnia.   Scented ambiance
of bazaars.   Difficult dialects.

Old men bent over silver designs.
Sinister Turkish tracing.   Patterns
of oppression.   Teutonic outrage.
Defiance.   Germane assassinations.

Raspoloženje:
childhood in maternal attics
paternal voices mutter, "Mirna
Bosna." To remedy a mad world
peace in Bosnia.

Sloboda.   Potreba.
Freedom as necessity. Fathomless
longing.   Justice.   Crystal pain
in slavic longitudes.

Ancestral demography.   A thirst
quenched on the sweet acids of
lemon.   We move from substance
into silence. Music of vivid
voices. History the murmur
which remains.

III

Improbable the juxtaposition of place.
Paradigm of significance.   Obscure
in a grassy side lane pointed toward
the Juan de Fuca Strait.   A stalwart
edifice to faith.   The church.

Small, Blue-domed.   Russian.
White-washed walls.   Orthodox.
Once a garage.   Now gardened.
The Czarist flag flies beside
the Union Jack.   Ikons of empire
in decline.

In the dusty cemeteries
of Bosnia stubborn graves.   Bogumel.
These Christian heretics compete
with the bayonet dazzle
of Minarets: Begova Dzamije.

Above the pointed poplars circular
the kestrel hawk flies.   Swallows
stammer in the pointed aspens. A bell
chimes.

Serenely temporal the Russian
church dreams.   Becalmed by
the western sea.   A window
on sorrow.

Raspoloženje.   Resonances
of geography merging into
mythology.   History.
Making of summer's fire
and winter's indelible ice
an element true
as air, older
than desire.

from
WHITE LINEN
REMEMBERED
(1996)

Vinka

or The Fabric of Legend

Gentle reader this tale
    improbable as it may
    read is true.

In a hot implacable August
    on a small island
    in a smaller village
    these events occurred.

At dawn my uncle
    wakes me to the sight
    and sound of the sea
    seraphic on the nearby shore.

Gently I am placed
    on his household vehicle
    a patient elderly donkey.

Today is the day we visit
    Great Aunt Vinka in the hills
    beyond Great St. Nikola.

We climb steeply
    into those hills filled
    with the scent of heaven
    wild thyme redolent rosemary.

Below us the Adriatic
    preens in the morning air
    by the wayside lemon trees
    compete with wild oak

Each soothed by
        the constant syllabic hum
        of mourning doves the startled
        slither of hares in the limestone outcrop.

The path leads
        to a clearing where wild olives
        back against a stone ascent
        of clambering cliff.

Sovereign in the door
        of a dim oracular cave
        dressed in black so worn
        it shines grey white

Tall and gaunt
        as her gnarled olive grove
        spindle in her hand
        stands my great aunt, Vinka.

A woman grown
        not old but ancient
        as temple ruins and crumpled
        city walls are ancient.

Matriarchal she bends
        to bless me looks direct
        unequivocal into my startled
        eyes. She nods recognition.

The air stunned
        into silence by the heat
        of noon is punctured by
        the rasp of cicadas.

And our formal halting greetings.

She looms before us
    the village sybil, healer
    and seer, the clairvoyant
    voice of augury.

Before speaking she smiles
    her mouth free of teeth
    is generous with portent
    the power of utterance.

Her voice is silver
    a silver thread in a fabled
    morning as the spindle she holds
    is mythic with the power
    to weave legend.

We give her honey
    bread with goat's cheese
    a dark harsh wine
    red grapes, black olives.

I part with her reluctant
    leaving behind devoted
    a particle of memory
    enshrined forever votive
    in my future mind.

As we leave
    she calls after me, "Little niece
    comfort yourself with singing
    for you will not be happy
    until late in life."

We move downward
> the sardonic Adriatic sun
> beats a bruise of heat
> into our shelterless backs.

All this was in another country.

I comfort myself with singing.

White Linen Remembered

"Tamo daleko . . ."

I
CODES TO EXISTENCE

If all manner of things
are to be well,
are to be well remembered,
as flowers are codes, birds
alphabets to existence

then childhood
is white linen. White linen
cross-stitched with crimson. With
petals. Flowers abstracted.

Gardens are roses. Carnations
and camomile. Rosemary.
The grass sprinkled with thyme.
Border fragrance. Lavender.
The scent fond. Remembering.

Soft speech. Strangers
framed in doorways.
The custom of courtesy.
Wine served. The best.
In the Sunday glass.

My father present
in absence. Counterpoint
of names which nourish
the folklore of fishing,
fables of origin. Namu.
Mostar. Rivers Inlet.
Vis. Seymour Narrows.
Sarajevo. Hecate Strait.

Hecate, goddess
of crossings. Shadows.
We left behind in an
abandoned convent. Haunted
by ghosts of misplaced nuns.

Friends come. In the early
grace of the day's time. Large
corded men. Civil with
laughter. Welcome the dower
white linen of olive dark
women.

Sunlight on stone. Leeside
we shelter. Catch at confidences.
The harbour at Hvar. Olive
and lemon grove. Tapestry
of shared affection. Komiža.
Ancestral fig tree. Prophetic
Nis. Skull tower. Ohrid.
Angelic fresco.

II
THE LIME TREE

I pause. Bemused by traffic.
On a prosperous thoroughfare. Stand
in a shop. Listen to the simmer
of shoppers. Shopkeeper's talk.

Hear the familiar: the language.
Dialect maternal
accent paternal
content inimical.

Unwilling the ear records
faction. Small mean
hate. Malice of region
erupts in the spittle of failed
fascists. Love of commerce
not kindred. The remaining
rancid rampart of the blessed:
the Croatian bourgeoisie.

Hint of contempt
in the price of purchase
black grapes green olives.
Homage to Dalmatia
not Ustasha madness.

Accidental as pleasure. A lime
tree planted. Grown for fidelity.
Love of the allusive. Fitful
years later. Learn it sacred.
Sacred in Serbia.

Expansive with summer
the leaves fill the garden
face the salt
of the sea. Acknowledge
Eastern approaches to history.
The hard red star. Resistance.

The silt of iron settles
in the mouth of the river.
Olive dark the women,
ceremony of stitches
finished. Wither.

My father vatic traverses
the straights of narrowed
passage. My mother
elemental dissolves
into sea mist. The red
star rides on the tide
elegiac.

Hobotniča

The Octopus

I

The old ghosts
          mourn.
The young cry
        out
their grief. Bitter
harvest at the end
of summer. Apples
of discord chewed
by black teeth.

I recall
my mother
leaning
on a withered
wooden fence.
Her kerchief
like the fabric
of her country
        torn.

She speaks
of her youth.
How as a very
young girl, a child
        almost
she walked
to the sea
at the end
of her garden.

Walked to where
in the clear
water swam
the octopus, the innocent
    hobotniča.

She dips
a dazzle
of white linen
into the pristine blue
    of the Adriatic
making a blaze
of whiteness
enticing the pink
    and white
sea creature
into its milky
    folds.

Artless
he swims
into the crystal
cream of its weave.

Triumphant
she holds him
    fast.
Ties a swift
    knot.
Takes him home
for the family
    evening meal.

II

Later
much later
she moves to a distant
                harbour
Rests the weight
of her pain
on clinical linen.

One dawn
a grave celebrant
expected, solicitous
lays on the lap
of her years
a length of bleached
                cloth
enticing this pink
                and grey
land creature
into the blanched small bones
of his stone embrace.

            White
on blue I shroud
her in my father's
colours. In the green
of grape leaves, the purple
pall of vineyards. Gold
for the light on the Adriatic.

                    Adieu
to both. Last stars
lost stars. I hear
you in the hour
of vespers. See
you move past
the thuggish dissonance
of present history
into the bold eye
of the clear
                    morning.

Noctis Equi

Toward dawn
I hear the relentless beat
the thud and thunder
of their hard feet.

They are not slow
these horses of the night.
No impulse from my troubled
sleep murmurs, *lente, lente,*
to those hooves of approaching
                          grief.

They race across
remote terrain morosely
swift violent
nostrils distended
with omens
ill of will.

Frozen in nightmare
I wince nor can I
speak meshed in a terror
as prehistoric as the hulk
of grazing mammoths
who chew on crimes
in the dead light.

In that dead light
the voice of Faustus
shrieks for but one drop
for half a saving drop.

Ovid appears, lunar
Ovid grim in exile
betrayed by fatal fidelity
the need to write consummately
of the erotic itch.

I struggle with disordered
sheets. Catch at the curtains.
Reach for the branch
                of morning.

An open window reaffirms
the absolutes lost to night:

A knowledge of warm
flat rocks facing the sea

green cold water
on a hot day

sunlight after rain
a gull's white wing.

The five simple senses
revived by a fragrant breeze
hear the bird of dawning.
Ordinary daylight suggests
beatitude, the possibles
                of blessedness.

The Shadow Self

I reach out
I chant the runes
whisper prayers.
The shadow moves
it will not stay.

The man who comes
for daily bread
refuses wine.

His shadow self
dissolves and fades
will not pause
    at the open gate.

I grasp for hands
touch broken bones.

They sing in my ears
discords of song.

Shadow shadow
on the wall
who's the darkest
one of all?

The sky recedes
the earth retreats
the wind blows chill.

Who knocks at the door?
What knocks at the window pane?

The shadow man
with a pail of crumbs
the shadow man
who will not talk.

Like a dry leaf
in a harsh light

he drops, he drops.

Matrona Luminosa

When I am old
and half asleep drowsing
over old fidelities
I shall move
toward the wisdom
found in the sound
        of water.

Visit in spirit
Parry Falls
where the numinous woman
lives wrapped in a silver net
        of spray
behind walls of falling water.

Driven by outrage
intrepid with anger
embittered she leaves
her people retreats
        into water.

The village shaman
solicitous to repair
injury transforms into a
        striated wasp
flies behind the waterfall
offers conciliation
petitions forgiveness.

Reconciliation accomplished
he leaves.
She remains
a titular deity to
the face of water.

Silence follows
measured by the thaw
of numb arctic devotion.

Above the virtues
of the star-lit heavy
wingèd seraphim descend
as heavenly servants
to mortal manifestation
of the immortal:
the illuminated,
the woman,
Matrona luminosa.

Ancient hierarchies of grace
resonate knowing.
Relate legends of the luminous
the shining woman resplendent
in the concentric circles
        of myth.

Revealing the iridescent
mysteries of pattern
of redemption in the ripples
of moonlight on water
in the voice of the river
a distant view of the sea.

The Altered Air

At the far edge
of the creek I see
the final bloom of summer
in the green salal, the amber
             of water.

A child sings
where the sand is wet.
Two women read
in the shade of a rowan
             tree.

Deep in the hectic
red of ripening berries
they sit to read
at peace with mind
             and matter.

Miraculously free from electronic noise
the nubile young doze
on the hot rocks of late
             afternoon.

At the quiet end
of evening mist moves
unravelling into the west.

A light breeze
absolves the heat-dependent
day's obsession.

Drift-net gulls
their wings turned toward
autumn hover above the transparent
promise of legend.

Perfect harbingers
they offer gifts,
a season of cucumbers
a feast of altered air.

A Mandala of Birds
and Feathers

The unexpected felicity
of the heron propped
solitary by the irrigation pump.

The white-washed lace of ice
on a waste of wide water.

Black quail nimble
in the frozen orchard.

A mandala of birds and feathers
as visiting finch perch

on the mustard radiance
of a winter willow.

Chill wind, hoarfrost
last words spoken

on a walk from southern darkness
into the migratory northern light.

Joseph Plaskett Sketching

He stands absorbed
   an abstract in a line
   of trees.
Intent on the lake
   he sketches.

Committed citizen
   of the imagination
   comely as courtesy.
Poised in the politesse of old
                  civilizations.
Partial to soft declensions
               slow desuetudes.

Watch as he leans
in the crook of the
               road.
Practised to rescue
the fading afternoon
   from anonymity.

Circles and Painted Horses

In Memoriam
Ralph Gustafson

".. . *The painted horse*
goes into that darkness where all circles go. "
PATRICK LANE

The painted horse. Darkness.
I write of concentric circles
turning into light. Summer
grief turns those circles dark.

My circles spin. A vatic silence
speaks to the poet of the carousel.
He draws those sinuous charts
of darkness where all circles
go. His painted horse faithful
as the sun returning after rain
emerges grave with augury.

In childhood
I loved cold. Longed for
the inviolates of snow. Evening
ultimates of violet light. Now
late and large in life I know
the harder core of ice.

Old friends
clear in the heart and dear
as the bells of morning climb
the painted horses. Ride soft
eyed into galactic distance.

Leave me to gaze
at mullioned windows. Lookouts
of memory. Framed by the lattice
of time shared. Windows lit
by the flicker of a heart bright
with the patina of farewell.

Slow horse. Fading
anchored rider. Reins restive with
longing for pattern. Design to defeat
depredation. Respond to the silver
of water. The firm earth of healing.
Green gratitude in the arms of sleep.

NEW POEMS

Visible Living

The natural prayer
    of the soul
wrote Rilke of poetry.

The sky moves
the grass grasps
my outstretched fingers.

I hear the measured
    rhythm
of ordinary breathing.
The soul at rest
in the silence between
    syllables.

Alone at the sea's edge
I escape into the cadence
of language in love
with visible living.

Timeless Healing

I live with hemlock and cedar.
You wanted fig trees
oleander and kiwi fruit.
You had them in your patio garden.

In the recesses of the heart
dedicated to perfection
you planted hibiscus.
I wanted daisies and tiger lilies.

Farewell, I give you up
to timeless healing
dreams of Adriatic water
we shared when young.

Sleep and leave the tumult
the search for balance
the lift of the eye deciphering
heaven from earth.

The stars tumble
helter skelter in your manic
laughter. Something cosmic
mutters in your mouth
prophetic of pain to come.

Wake in the dreamless sphere
of music. Reverberations
of innocent harmonics.
The mind at rest in measureless
repose without clocks or shadows.

Three Peonies

The edict issued
was for flowers.

Flowers to be held
in a clasped reverence
of hands.

The procession to wind
through the narrow
perspective of the faded church.

No flowers in her mother's
garden will suffice.
The neighbour's plot
offers peonies. Great
globular discs, petals tight
against the drenching rain.

She walks across
a squelch of lawn
reaches for the stalks, breaks three,
runs hasty with guilt
into the parallel street.

Inside the church
at the top of the steep
hill, she breathes
in the pungency of incense.

Kneels in the aisle
fingers bent hard
on the stolen peony blooms.

Three peonies clutched
in a small fist
of necessity to believe
to belong to the warmth
to confirm the beatitude
feel the ecstatic reprieve
assured by the beatific
flame, the white radiance
at the core of the sanctified heart.

In the heated church
and the healing balm
of her hands
the peony flowers expand
the pristine petals part.

Eyes focused on the central
core of the flower
pale pure petal touched
with pink, she observes
a swirl of dark
a writhing cluster
of black agitated ants.

Singularity

Two by two
the companionable geese
like the wild swans at Coole
    swim.

In sombre pairs
committed to fidelity
these birds pass by
and float on the brim
    of tidal water.

They are brown and black
not ethereal white.

They do not soar
above the froth
of the incoming tide.

I hear a voice
on the opposite shore cry,
"My grandmother's kettle
sick in my grandmother's kettle."

Old miseries from other times
not mine, another's.
Now exorcised
by happy expanded lives.

The mountains behind
turn a naval blue.
The geese paddle;
I swim the crest
of a brusque impatient wave.

Companionable geese
swans at Coole
images of absence at evening
crowd the retinas
of my striving eyes.

I walk into the green
of the forest path

say a wet farewell
to the near happiness
of scattered seashells.

Distant and uphill
the empty house
waits for my return
to the hard mysteries
    of singularity.

Of Mary and the Sickle Moon

I

A careful parent sent me
shy and awkward
barely speaking English
to a parochial convent school.

There various snub-nosed
sometimes blue often green-eyed
Irish-Canadian girls could not
pronounce my name.

They were not hostile
nor contemptuous, merely
perplexed or exasperated,
these Eileen O'Briens and Sheila O'Neils.

They dubbed me, inappropriately,
Mary, not Marya, not Fiamengo
but From England. Mary From England.

Blithely impervious to that Adriatic
littoral, my ancestral geographic home.
I calmly accepted the nomenclature
eventually growing out of Mary
into Marya not From England but Fiamengo.

II

And as I grew I mused
on various Marys and their fates.
The Marys I met in my reading
in the restricted convent library.

Chiefly, Royal Marys. Mary Stuart
Queen of Scots, her youth eaten up
by plots and Elizabethan prisons,
notorious Fotheringhey castle where
she was sorely tried and executed.

Tragic Mary Tudor in love
with her Spanish blood and her
cold Spanish husband. Not lily
tall, amber of eye and hair, the slender
stellar brilliant Elizabeth, but short,
near-sighted, domestic by nature, and
kind. Made miserable by the blood
shed in her name. Adamantly
Catholic, fiercely devout.

Mary, Mary, quite contrary,
How does your garden grow?
With silver bells and cockle shells,
And heretics all in a row.

Mary Tudor who thought she was
pregnant, died of a tumor. She
wanted Philip of Spain and connubial
domestic life, Philip and history
decreed otherwise.

III

Mary listed in the dictionary of given
names means in Latin: star of the sea;
in Hebrew: bitter herb or our rebellion.
Therein lies the dual crux:
    Tower of gold
    Gate of Ivory
    Star of the Sea
sings the litany of the Blessed Virgin.
Mary of Guise, mother of Mary Queen
of Scots, Mary Tudor, Mary Magdalene.
Mary of France, sister to Henry VIII,
married politically expedient Louis XII,
sixty years older, widowed at eighteen,
defied Henry and France to marry miraculously
Charles Brandon, Duke of Suffolk,
a measure of happiness hazardly achieved.

Mary, more correctly Marie de la Incarnation,
Ursuline nun, superior of the convent
in Quebec, who worked with the French

missionaries in 1639, dedicated to God
not inquisitional fires.

All these Marys, some exemplary, some
not, lived hard exacting lives.

IV

A final image comes to mind,
the sickle moon madonna,
triumphant, enthroned in the crescent
moon, the radiant child deity
in her arms. Her heel crushes
the phallic serpent head.

The ultimate Mary.
Beyond the reach of flesh and bone
stands alone in the dark sky
a single star at the edge
of her crescent luminous throne.

Now I walk at night
beneath an altered moon,
Diana's moon, sometimes auspicious,
sometimes not. Mary, *ad Mare*
of the sea, the ebb and flow
of tides. Of feet walking on
the rough pebbled shore.
Walking no longer blithe and bonnie
and of England or the Adriatic littoral
but inward toward
an increasingly advancing final shore.

Of Warriors and Blessing

Two women
in the calm of the
        evening.
The room is still.
They sit quiet with
the full repositories
        of their years.

They listen
as music spills old
        legends
into the crystalline air.

The music sings
of a white birch tree.
Asks of the quiescent
        night
is it the slender white
of the birch tree
that sways in the
        autumn wind?

The night replies,
No, it is not the white
        birch tree.
It is the lithe young
        bones
of the young warrior
as he bows before
        his welcoming mother.

He asks her blessing
before the dissonance of
                    battle
shatters the sweet harmony
of music and peace.

He speaks
and his ardent syllables
reach the tender reception
of old ears.

Farewell, dearest mother,
Farewell, much loved sister.
Remember as I go to battle
that when I die
I die because I love you.

II

The white birch trembles
the sun fading glitters
on the white hair
of the women, grave
with the weight of years.

The young warrior bowing,
the old women seated.
Beyond the window
the wheat field ripens
the gracious grass grows
as an evening bell rings
a full moon shines
on courage and virtue.

The old women smile
the young warrior caresses
dream and desire
the birch tree bends
under the night sky
rich with stars and benediction.

Insoluble Movement

The east wind blows.
Cherry and apple bloom.
May once again.
It is morning,
doves from the Okanagan
fly through the mind.

May poles. Fertility dance.
The doves arrive
with dead twigs
in their beaks.

Chill in the air.
I sit cold
a stone on my heart
pebbles of sorrow
on my tongue
requiem of regret
in my head.

In a cloud of insoluble
movement two transparent
friends ascend.

Memory laid out
washed and wrapped in linen.

Directions

At a loss
for direction
unable to read
    the street signs
I stop to feed birds
talk to green trees
resist erosion
the malice of the small
    mean hour.

What comfort
in the riddle of pillows?

The hard insistent
inevitables arrive.

Cold rain
and daylight.

I want the dark
dreamless sleep
without brittle stars
or the sly whispering
moon telling me lies.

At the Edge

Now that I seldom sing
now that there is a constant
humming in my ears
hymns throbbing in my head

I remember the walk west
along the solitary tree thick road

above the sea
and the muted mumble
of insistent traffic.

It was March
the air was white
with blessings of bloom to come
where I half saw
half heard the hum
of powerful wings.

We had laid you down
with earth and flowers
dutiful obsequies done.
I walked to ease the hurting
the handful of relinquished dust.

To the left of my eye
parallel in the visible
retina of sight
suspended unfaltering
the eagle flew
alongside.

I paused,
the bird floated, glided, hovered
above me, beyond me, by me
a passing shadow of feather
across my darkened brow.

It dipped in a moment
of grace, it soared to answer
the transparent breath
from my throat.

Ascent aslant the last light
a rush of plumage
a freight of passage
falling into distance
toward the dying fire
the final harbinger
of harbour at the edge.

ABOUT THE AUTHOR

Marya Fiamengo was born in 1926 in Vancouver, British Columbia, the child of immigrants from the Croatian island of Vis. Her first language was Croatian, and the vocabulary and mythology of her ancestral land are a strong presence in her poetry. Complementing her Slavic roots is Fiamengo's love for the English language. She earned a Bachelor's degree in English from the University of British Columbia and a Master's degree in English and Creative Writing under the direction of Earle Birney and Dorothy Livesay. She taught in the English department at UBC from 1962 to 1993, publishing seven volumes of poetry as well as numerous critical reviews and essays. Since the early 1970s, she has been a passionate advocate of Canadian cultural and national autonomy. She now lives in Gibsons, BC, where she continues to write poetry and to lobby the government on issues of culture and social justice.